VIOLIN

SIMPLE LEARNING GUIDE

&

BASICS

IN CARNATIC STYLE

Vol 1

Ananthakrishnan .S.S

Peroorkada

To,

Common music

&

Violin lovers

Contents

1. Introduction

2. History

3. Parts of violin

4. Sitting position

5. Holding the bow

6. Bow practice

7. Mayamalavagowla raga

8. Miscellaneous songs

Introduction

This book is written in such a way that, I am trying my best to make the common people understand how they can play violin on their own, and to introduce them to some general information related to music and playing violin in Carnatic style.

As we all know music is like an ocean. Even I haven't touched its single drop yet. One must keep on learning to atleast get a drop of it. The things that I explain here is mainly based on playing violin in Carnatic style. As this is the first volume I introduce you to some of the most important topics related playing violin.

Ananthakrishnan.S.S

Peroorkada

History

The presence of instrument similar to violin was seen in early 14th and 15th centuries in western Europe and Egyptian civilization. The violin we see today was first introduced in 16th century by Andre Amati and Gasparodi Bertolotti in Northern Italy (Cremona).

The term violin came from the Italian word 'viol'. Amati's violin was so famous during that time that the reagent queen of France at that time bought Amati's violins and dedicated it for her son Charles IX. Hence the violins during that time was also known by his name.

Coming back to Carnatic music, the violin was introduced here for the first time by Baluswamy Dikshithar.

Parts of violin

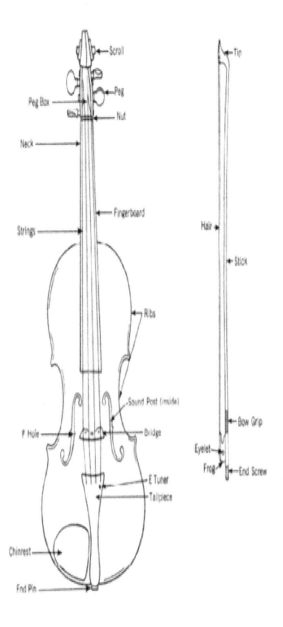

Sitting Position

The violin is placed between the neck and the side part of the heel as shown in figure. While sitting on the floor we must ensure that we sit in a straight posture and the upper body, the

leading leg and the violin must form a triangle.

Always make sure that the violin is held correctly to get the right hold.

Holding the bow

Once you place the violin properly, you must take the bow. While taking the bow ensure that you take it by placing your right hand's middle finger and thumb on the bow grip.

Obviously when you take like that, the tip part of the bow will fall towards the ground, here you will use your little finger to balance the bow keeping it straight by placing it near the screw part of the bow.

Never touch the hair part of the bow. The rest of the fingers must be placed on the stick part just as a support.

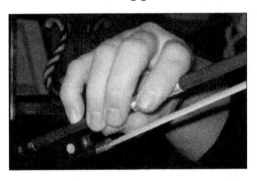

Bow practice

Once you are set with the violin and bow, the first thing one has to do is to tune the strings. For beginners and for practice I prefer to tune the strings to **C** or **D**. You can do it with the help of sruthi box or chromatic tuner.

Now the first thing you must do is to play each string moving the whole bow from bottom to tip part with the bow moving exactly between sound bridge and upper end of the finger board.

When you get that knack to play clearly, try to play the strings with top, middle and bottom part of the bow by partitioning it into three parts. After practicing in slow speeds, try to bow with maximum speeds you can.

Mayamalavagowla raga

In Carnatic music, whether it's vocal or instrument the first raga a beginner gets introduced to is Mayamalavagowla raga.

This raga has many aspects which makes it unique for basic learning. Its poorvardham and utharaardham are same. Which means the finger position for **Sa Ri Ga Ma** and **Pa Da Ni Sa'** are same. Now lets look its finger position in finger board.

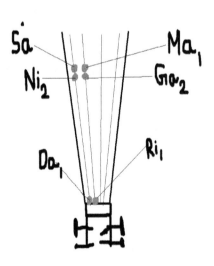

Here when you play second string starting from your right, you will get middle octave **Sa**, which is shadjam. Now using your left index finger press the second string are immediately after the nut. Here you get **Ri**, which is shudha rishabham.

Now just like how you roll your middle finger in your left palm and try to touch the skin area just below the thumb, try to do it with middle finger on the finger board in second string. It's **Ga,** which is gandharam.

And finally when place your left ring finger just above middle finger without any gap, you get **Ma,** which is madhyamam.

In the same way it you repeat it on first string starting from the left, you get **Pa, Da, Ni** and **Sa'**, which are panchamam, sudha daivatham, kakai nishadham and thara sthaayi shadjam.

This way you will be able to play the very fundamental of the raga in middle octave.

With middle octave you have to learn many swara combinations inorder to get finger flexibility. After that we go ahead like what we learn in vocal music, starting from sarali varisakal,janda varisakal etc.

After finishing till alankaras, you will be introduced to the main concept in Carnatic music, the Gamakams.

When you play a raga in gamakam only, it will get the real life. It takes time, but with interest and hard work one can surely succeed.

Miscellaneous songs

1. BETHLEHEMIL UNNI YESU PIRANNU

with notations

Bethlehemil, Unni Yesu, pirannu

Pa Ma Ga Ma, Pa Ma Ga Ma, Pa Ma Gaa

Bethlehemil, Unni Yesu, pirannu

Pa Ma Ga Ma, Pa Ma Ga Ma, Pa Ma Gaa

Yesu pirannu, Unni, Yesu pirannu

Sa Ga Ma Ga Sa, Sa Sa, Sa Ga Ma Ga Sa

Lokamaake, chaithanyam, pakaruvanaayi

**Pa Ma Ga Ma, Pa Ma Ga Ma, Pa
Sa'Sa'Sa'Saa'**

2. CHINGAM VANNE

with notations

Chingam, vanne, poovin

Pa Saa', Sa' Pa, Pa Pa

Atham, vanne, koode

Ga Maa, Ga Sa, Sa Sa

Maveli, rajavum

Sa Gaa Ma, Ga Maa Pa

Vannee, dunne

Pa Saa', Pa Saa'

Pookal, puthu, naatthil

Pa Saa', Sa' Pa, Pa Pa

Aakhoshamaayi, veettil

Ga Maa, Ga Sa, Sa Sa

Onathinolangal

Sa Gaa Ma, Ga Maa Pa

Veendum, Vanne

Pa Saa', Pa Saa'

3. RAMZAN RAAVU

with notations

Ramzan, pira, kandu

Sa Ma, Ga Ri, Sa Sa

Vishudhiyude, naalukal

SaSaaRiSaaSaa Rii Sa Sa

Ramzan, pira, kandu

Sa Ma, Ga Ri, Sa Sa

Vishudhiyude, naalukal

SaSaaRiSaaSaa Rii Sa Sa

Allaa, hu, Akbar

SaaMaa Gaa PaaMaMaa

Akabar, Allaa, hu, Akbar

PaMaGaRi SaRiiiSaa Sa RiSaaSaa

Rasoole, kaniyenam,

SaRiiRii SaRiSaaSaa

Rasoole, kaniyenam,

SaRiiRii SaRiSaaSaa

Rasoole, kaniyenam,

SaRiiRii SaRiSaaSaa

Rasoole, kaniyenam,

SaRiiRii PaMaRiiSaa

4. NAMMUDE BHARATAM

with notations

Bharatham, nammude, bhoomi

PaaMaGa, SaaSaSa, SaaSaa

Bharatham, nammude, bhoomi

PaaMaGa, SaaSaSa, SaaSaa

Vividha, Samskara, Sangama, Bhoomi

SaGaMa, MaaMaaMa, PaaPaPa, Saa'Saa'

Bharatham, nammude, bhoomi

PaaMaGa, SaaSaSa, SaaSaa

Bharatham, nammude, bhoomi

PaaMaGa, SaaSaSa, SaaSaa

Pathittandukalude, smaranakalurangum

PaMaGaaGaMaGaMa, SaGaMaGaSaSaSaa

Bharatham, nammude, bhoomi

PaaMaGa, SaaSaSa, SaaSaa

Bharatham, nammude, bhoomi

PaaMaGa, SaaSaSa, SaaSaa

Poralikalaal, Paduthuyarthiya

SaaGaaMaGaGaa, SaGa, SaGa, SaGa

Swathantra, bharata, bhoomi

GaMaaMa PaaPaPa Saa'Saa'

Jai Hind, Jai Hind, Jai Hind

PaaSa', PaaSa', PaaSa'

Jai Hind, Jai Hind

PaaSa', PaaSa'

5. <u>KEZHUNNA BHOOMI</u>

with notations

Piranna, bhoomi, naam, marannu

GaMaaGa, SaaSaa, Rii, SaRiSaa

Piranna, bhoomi, naam, marannu

GaMaaGa, SaaSaa, Rii, SaRiSaa

Vikasanathin, peril, naam

SaGaaMaaMaaMaa, GaaMaa, Paa

Bhoomiye, velluvilichu

GaaMaPa, DaaPaDaPaaPaa

Piranna, bhoomi, naam, marannu

GaMaaGa, SaaSaa, Rii, SaRiSaa

Piranna, bhoomi, naam, marannu

GaMaaGa, SaaSaa, Rii, SaRiSaa

Oduvil, athu, oduvil

GaMaPaa, GaMa, GaMaPaa

Pralayamaayi, kezhunivide

PaMaPaDaa, PaaMaaGaRiSaa

Piranna, bhoomi, naam, marannu

GaMaaGa, SaaSaa, Rii, SaRiSaa

Piranna, bhoomi, naam, marannu

GaMaaGa, SaaSaa, Rii, SaRiSaa

suggestions/feedbacks-

e-mail: ssa08945@gmail.com